#71
Westwood Branch
1246 Glendon Ave.
Los Angeles, CA 90024

W9-AVK-954

W9-BZP-266

HIP-HOP

Hip-Hop

Ludacris

Celicia Scott

Mason Crest Publishers

Ludacris

FRONTIS Ludacris has turned music success into an award-winning acting career, a successful business, and a foundation for doing good works.

PRODUCED BY 21ST CENTURY PUBLISHING AND COMMUNICATIONS, INC.

EDITORIAL BY HARDING HOUSE PUBLISHING SERVICES, INC.

MASON CREST PUBLISHERS INC.
370 Reed Road
Broomall, Pennsylvania 19008
(866)MCP-BOOK (toll free)
www.masoncrest.com

Printed in Malaysia.

First Printing

9 8 7 6 5 4 3 2 1

Library of Congress Cataloging-in-Publication Data

Scott, Celicia.
    Ludacris / by Celicia Scott.
      p. cm. — (Hip-hop)
    Includes index.
ISBN 1-4222-0122-8
    1. Ludacris (Rapper)—Juvenile literature. 2. Rap musicians—United States—Biography—Juvenile literature. I. Title. II. Series.
ML3930.L85S36 2007
782.421649092—dc22
[B]   2006010769

Publisher's notes:
• All quotations in this book come from original sources, and contain the spelling and grammatical inconsistencies of the original text.

• The Web sites mentioned in this book were active at the time of publication. The publisher is not responsible for Web sites that have changed their addresses or discontinued operation since the date of publication. The publisher will review and update the Web site addresses each time the book is reprinted.

Contents

Hip-Hop Timeline

1974 Hip-hop pioneer Afrika Bambaataa organizes the Universal Zulu Nation.

1988 *Yo! MTV Raps* premieres on MTV.

1970s Hip-hop as a cultural movement begins in the Bronx, New York City.

1985 *Krush Groove*, a hip-hop film about Def Jam Recordings, is released featuring Run-D.M.C., Kurtis Blow, LL Cool J, and the Beastie Boys.

1970s DJ Kool Herc pioneers the use of breaks, isolations, and repeats using two turntables.

1979 The Sugarhill Gang's song "Rapper's Delight" is the first hip-hop single to go gold.

1986 Run-D.M.C. are the first rappers to appear on the cover of *Rolling Stone* magazine.

1970   1980   1988

1976 Grandmaster Flash & the Furious Five pioneer hip-hop MCing and freestyle battles.

1986 Beastie Boys' album *Licensed to Ill* is released and becomes the best-selling rap album of the 1980s.

1970s Break dancing emerges at parties and in public places in New York City.

1982 Afrika Bambaataa embarks on the first European hip-hop tour.

1988 Hip-hop music annual record sales reaches $100 million.

1970s Graffiti artist Vic pioneers tagging on subway trains in New York City.

1984 *Graffiti Rock*, the first hip-hop television program, premieres.

1993 Rapper Snoop Dogg's album *Doggystyle* is the first debut album to hit the music charts at number one.

2006 Queen Latifah becomes the first hip-hop artist to receive a star on the Hollywood Walk of Fame.

1989 DJ Jazzy Jeff & The Fresh Prince become the first hip-hop artists to win a Grammy Award.

2003 Rapper Eminem becomes the first hip-hop artist to win an Academy Award.

2005 Hip-hop artist Kanye West appears on the cover of *Time* magazine.

1989 Rap is added as a new category to the *Billboard* charts.

1997 East Coast rapper Notorious B.I.G. (aka Biggie Smalls) is murdered.

2004 First National Hip-Hop Political Convention is held in Newark, New Jersey.

1989   2000   2006

1990s Hip-hop emerges in Europe.

1996 West Coast rapper Tupac Shakur is shot and killed.

2005 Rapper Will Smith opens the Philadelphia Live 8 concert as part of 10 simultaneous concerts held worldwide to bring attention to the extreme poverty in Africa.

1989 First gangsta rap album, *Straight Outta Compton*, is released by N.W.A.

2001 The hip-hop political action group, Hip-Hop Summit Action Network, is founded by Russell Simmons.

1992 Dr. Dre's album *The Chronic* is released; it redefines West Coast rap.

2006 The Smithsonian Institute National Museum of American History announces the creation of a new hip-hop exhibition scheduled to open in three to five years.

Ludacris doesn't pull any punches in his music. Though his lyrics can cause big-name corporations to back away from his potential as a spokesperson, his millions of fans find his Dirty South hip-hop music something to which they can relate.

◀ 1 ▶

Not Afraid of Controversy

He raps about sex, drugs, and violence. His lyrics are explicit and often **controversial**. His uncompromising style has **garnered** the wrath of high-profile individuals such as Bill O'Reilly and lost him endorsement deals with huge companies like Pepsi. He has also sold more than twelve million albums, earned millions of loyal fans, and helped define an entire **genre** of music.

Ludacris, a hip-hop artist from Atlanta, Georgia, burst into the music world in 2000. His rhymes reflect the gritty urban world, racked by poverty and racism, that gave rise to hip-hop culture. But his lyrics often have a lighter side as well. Although Ludacris raps plenty about the drugs and violence that are prominent in the hip-hop world, he is famous for his songs about "the ladies." Not that this makes him any less controversial. The explicit—some would say vulgar—rhymes about women and sex that define his music have been credited by some as putting the "dirt" in the Dirty South hip-hop scene.

Hip-Hop: Born in the Bronx

Hip-hop is an urban cultural movement defined by music, art, and dance. It began in the 1970s in the Bronx in New York City. At that time, the African American and Latino communities there began experimenting with new ways of expressing themselves and critiquing their often-harsh world. This expression manifested in a new form of music called rap, art called graffiti or tagging, and dance called b-boying or break dancing.

The hip-hop cultural revolution was carried out to a large extent by young people in public spaces. Visually, individuals and groups created

A common sign of hip-hop culture is graffiti. In cities all over America, artists have "tagged" walls, subway and railway cars, and almost anything else with large, colorful images. Some see graffiti as harmless self-expression, but others believe it should be cleaned off immediately.

In hip-hop's early days, young boys could be seen break dancing—or b-boying—on street corners in the Bronx and other New York City locations. It was another way that young people found to express themselves.

an art form by tagging the places they had been or the terrain they claimed; their graffiti was painted on buildings, buses, bridges, and other public structures. Musically, rapping and b-boying began in the clubs but moved to the streets. There, young men would use their mouths and bodies to do battle for respect and territory.

Today, we think of gangs battling with guns, but in the 1970s, rap and break dancing became ways for young men to show their skills, "fight" their opponents, and gain followers. This is not to say, however, that rapping and dancing replaced violence in the streets. They did not. But they became extremely important parts of street culture and gave birth to what we know today as hip-hop. Hip-hop culture is now influential all over the world and can be seen not only in the popular music that defines it, but also in the fashion, language, and other cultural elements it has inspired.

The Anatomy of Hip-Hop Music

Hip-hop music is unique in the musical world, perhaps most notably because it does not use traditional musicians or instruments. In fact, when hip-hop was first developed, it did not use "original" musical scores at all, and much hip-hop still does not today. Instead, the music of hip-hop was created by a **DJ** using songs that already existed. The DJ is accompanied by an **MC** who raps to the music the DJ creates.

To create the music, the DJ isolates the song's breaks, the portion of the music that contains the beat. Originally, these breaks were isolated from **funk** and disco songs, but today they are also commonly taken from rock, **soul**, and other hip-hop songs. The DJ then takes the isolated breaks, usually two of them, and plays them simultaneously, manipulating them to create a new sound. Traditionally, this is done using two turntables (a record on each turntable), and basic equipment including a **mixer**, amplifier, and speakers.

In the early days of hip-hop, the DJs were the stars of the music. Their practice of isolating breaks and turntabling has its roots in Jamaican music and was further developed in New York City clubs and at block parties. At these **venues**, the goal was to keep the partygoers dancing, and the DJs knew the breaks were the most danceable parts of the songs. By isolating the breaks and keeping them playing, the audience could continue dancing uninterrupted. A good DJ was much appreciated and respected by the audience.

The DJ's role has changed over the years. Hip-hop songs are now created in studios and played over the radio. Having a good DJ at a club is still important, but technology has changed much about the creation and playing of hip-hop music. Today much of the hip-hop music, especially "pop hip-hop" uses instrumentals and **synthesizers** to create the beats rather than isolating the breaks of existing songs. As a result, the role of the live DJ is greatly diminished.

Today, the focus of hip-hop music is on the MC. In the early days of hip-hop, the MC had a secondary role; he introduced the DJ and kept the crowd entertained during breaks between songs. But the MCs quickly expanded their position, adding jokes, commentary, and ultimately delivering beat-driven performances. Their crowd-pleasing phrasing **melded** with the music and became increasingly elaborate. The use of rhyme became a focal point of the MC's performance, and what emerged was known as rapping. Rapping usually consists not

DJs were the first real hip-hop stars. DJs turned the turntable into a musical instrument, doing whatever was necessary to get a good dance beat. Technology has limited the DJ's role now, though he can still be an important fixture at a party.

only of rhyming but also of assonance—the repeated use of vowel sounds—and alliteration—using a string of words that all begin with the same consonant.

Although not one of its defining elements, beatboxing, creating drum- and bass-like beats using only the human voice, is also an important part of hip-hop music. A skilled beatboxer can provide the entire percussion portion of a song using no other instrument than a set of vocal chords. A group of beatboxers providing the music for a skilled MC's rhymes creates a sound like no other. Beatboxing faded from prominence for many years, but it is currently enjoying a **renaissance** in urban music the world over.

Reborn in the "Dirty" South

Today, hip-hop music comes in many forms and styles, and its artists are usually influenced by the regions and cultures in which they were raised, leading to significant differences in musical styles. For much of hip-hop's history, there was a rivalry between the East Coast style and West Coast style. Then a southern style began to emerge, and popularity increased for this new style developing in U.S. cities like Miami, Houston, Memphis, Atlanta, and New Orleans.

The southern style of rap was recognized by its dance-friendly beats and relatively simplistic, chanting rhythms. As had happened originally with hip-hop, it gained popularity in clubs because it was so danceable. Today, southern rap is perhaps the most popular form of hip-hop.

In the late 1990s, southern rap gave birth to yet another style of hip-hop, called Dirty South. The Dirty South style, in addition to being characterized by the upbeat rhythms that define the genre, is recognizable above all for its highly sexual lyrics. In addition, profanity, violence, and drugs all feature dominantly in Dirty South music, making it similar in content to gangsta rap, another extremely popular hip-hop form.

The term Dirty South also refers to a historical region of the United States, the Deep South. In that sense, the word "dirty" has more to do with the South's history of racially motivated oppression, legal corruption, and criminal activities.

Controversy with a Message

Today, Ludacris is one of the most successful Dirty South rappers. He's also one of the most controversial names in the hip-hop world.

Despite his success—or perhaps *because* of it—Ludacris is one of hip-hop's most controversial stars. And it's not just his lyrics people complain about. His performances and clothes have also been criticized. Ludacris insists, however, there is a message behind his choices.

At the 2005 VIBE awards, Ludacris performed wearing a replica of the Confederate flag. As he had expected, many were outraged. But Ludacris had a reason for wearing it: the flag represented oppression felt by African Americans for many years.

His lyrics, performances, and even at times the clothes that he wears, routinely cause debate and bring criticism. For example, at the 2005 VIBE Awards, Ludacris performed wearing a depiction of the Confederate flag, something that sat poorly with many people, especially many of his African American fans.

Ludacris may cause controversy with his music and performances, but he says he doesn't stir up controversy without a reason. He claims that a lot of thought goes into the decisions he makes about the things he says, the actions he takes, even the clothes he wears. When he does something that stimulates a strong reaction, Ludacris feels he's done something right.

The dispute his actions at the 2005 VIBE Awards generated is a perfect example. Ludacris later explained the thinking behind his actions. He stated in a press release:

> **"The discussions that have been sparked after my performance of 'Georgia' at the 2005 VIBE Awards is my exact reason for wearing a depiction of the Confederate Flag. This flag represents the oppression that we as African Americans have endured for years; this is a symbol of segregation and the racism that reigned not only throughout the South but throughout the entire United States. I wore it to represent where we came from, to remind people that Ray Charles's original 'Georgia' was written because of that racism."**

For Ludacris, it is extremely important that African American people, and all people, remember the history behind their lives and music. The music of the past and of the present often carries a message, and Ludacris doesn't want the messages of music from the past to be forgotten or the messages of today's music to be overlooked. His actions at the VIBE Awards were meant to remind people of the message about racism carried in the song "Georgia." But they had another purpose as well. They were also to make people think about the threat that racism continues to have today. In the interview, Ludacris explained this further saying:

> **"At the end of the performance, I removed and stomped on the flag to reveal my version of the flag; a flag comprised of black, red, and green. Those are the colors of Africa. It is a representation and my interpretation of where we were and where we need to go. Racism is just as prevalent now, and if we are not constantly mindful of our history and take charge of it, history is destined to repeat itself because of ignorance. In order to move forward, we must never forget where we were."**

More to the Music

The biggest controversy Ludacris faces, however, is the daily debate surrounding his music. His lyrics are filled with profanity, explosive sexual fantasies, and gritty themes. His music is often pointed to as a **quintessential** example of the Dirty South style. But one cannot be a thriving Dirty South artist without having to face the flip side that comes with success in the genre: the questions and criticisms that participating in such an explicit art form brings.

Ludacris's music has brought him many fans, but for every fan of Dirty South rap, there is a person who questions the **legitimacy** and morality of the musical form. They claim that Dirty South rap,

Ludacris's music has introduced many to the Dirty South style of hip-hop. Though some write off his music as just encouraging more violence and woman-hating, his millions of fans disagree. And Ludacris loves his fans. Here he signs autographs before a 2006 concert.

and often all hip-hop, is just a vehicle for violent, **chauvinistic**, **materialistic**, and criminal men to gain wealth and power and lure vulnerable young minds. They believe that hip-hop music and artists like Ludacris are bad influences on their generally young audience and can even be dangerous.

While many people focus on the profanity and seemingly glorified violence in hip-hop music, artists like Ludacris claim that there is much more to their art form than the shock value of the language. Although some hip-hop artists, specifically some in the genre of gangsta rap, do fit the violent, even criminal profile, Ludacris does not. He is generally known for being soft spoken. Unlike many hip-hop artists, he has never been in a gang, and he is deeply concerned about social issues and at-risk youth.

Artists who defend hip-hop say that not only are many among their ranks concerned about bettering the world as Ludacris is, theirs is also a socially conscious art form. It expresses the harsh realities that many people, particularly African Americans and Latinos, are forced to live with in a nation still defined by racism, poverty, and class divisions. Hip-hop music gives power and a voice to a huge population of **marginalized** people who would otherwise be powerless and voiceless. Defenders of hip-hop also say the music isn't creating a vulgar, violent, dangerous society; it is expressing a social reality that already exists but that many critics just prefer not to acknowledge.

Whether one likes it or hates it, believes it's powerful or degrading, hip-hop music is certainly filled with uncensored emotion. Ludacris says of his music, "I'm just basically spillin' out my emotions to the world, 'cause rap is about emotion. And I want you to feel what I'm feelin', 'cause that's what it's all about." Ludacris has spilled his emotions out to the world, and millions of fans have embraced him.

Growing up, Chris Bridges could always count on his mom for love and support. That is still true today. In this photo, Ludacris and his mom, Roberta Shields, attend the 2005 premiere of the Oscar-winning film *Crash*.

2

Becoming Chris Lova Lova

Ludacris may be a **platinum**-selling artist now, but he began with humble roots and a different name. Nevertheless, from the time he was a very small child, he knew what he wanted to be: a rapper, an MC. He wrote his first rhymes at nine years old—and he hasn't stopped since.

Ludacris's musical education began when he was very young. Born Christopher Bridges on September 11, 1977, in Champaign, Illinois, music was a defining part of his life from the very beginning. His parents were young when he was born, still just in college, and they included their son in the activities of college life. One of those activities was house **jams**. Chris says of those early years:

"[My parents] were always jamming to the old school stuff, like Frankie Beverly and Maze, Cameo, all that kind of music. They used to take me to college parties and let me get out in the middle of the floor and dance for all the other students."

But those carefree days wouldn't last forever. Eventually, Chris's parents split up, and although he experienced plenty of love and emotional support as a child, he also faced his share of hardship. As a single parent, his mother at times struggled to support them. But music was always something Chris could turn to for comfort.

A Born Rapper

Chris couldn't remember a time when he didn't want to rap. And he was never shy about performing either. Creating rhymes and spitting them out for his audience (his family and friends) came as naturally to Chris as things like baseball, bike riding, or jumping rope come to other children his age. For Chris, rapping was like playing; it was something he just loved to do. In an interview with AskMen.com, he recalled:

> **"When I was in middle school I always used to love listening to rap. The first [song] my pops bought me was U.T.F.O's 'Roxanne, Roxanne.' So ever since I was about five or six years old, I just liked listening to it. Then, when I was about eight or nine, I kinda started doing it for friends in middle school. They like hearing it. They wanted to hear more, so that's what motivated me to keep doing it."**

Though he admits the rhymes he made when he was nine years old were a little clumsy, they got him started on his passion; clearly, he had talent even at this young age. He wasn't even a teenager when he joined his first hip-hop group, the Chicago-based Loudmouth Hooligans. Chris was just twelve years old and already displaying the commitment and determination that would one day lead him to fame.

Soon after joining the Loudmouth Hooligans, Chris had to leave them to move to Atlanta. At his new school, College Park's Banneker High School, Chris again made a name for himself by rapping for his classmates. He rapped in the lunchroom and even challenged other classmates to MC battles. These schoolhouse competitions were good practice, because in just a few years Chris began going to talent shows and open mics.

Life in Atlanta

Although there were plenty of good times during Chris's teenage years in Atlanta, there were difficult ones as well. His mother kept him grounded and stressed the importance of education and responsibility. In an interview with the *San Francisco Chronicle*, Chris talked about the hard times he and his mother went through, and how she kept him moving in a positive direction. He recalled:

Chris loved rap from his youngest days. An early favorite of his was U.T.F.O., which stood for Untouchable Force Organization. The four members of the group met as dancers for another artist, Whodini, and went on to be stars in their own right.

"[T]here was a time when I had to live with my mom in one room in somebody else's house, so I know what it's like to struggle. I grew up street-smart and tried to do good in school at the same time. My mom was very strict; she disciplined me, taught me a lot about bank accounts, about saving money."

These were lessons Chris took seriously. When graduation time came, he had a difficult decision to make. Many people trying to break into the music business forgo education to follow their dream. But Chris's family had always stressed education's importance. Furthermore, no matter how talented a person is, the chances of succeeding in the cutthroat music industry are slim. Chris knew he would be wise to have an education to fall back on if that big break never came.

Chris decided to go to college, and use his education to help him succeed in the music world. Although he wanted to be a rapper, Chris also had a businessman's mind. He decided the best way to pursue his career was to get a degree in music management. He attended Georgia State University and developed the business know-how he needed.

Becoming Chris Lova Lova

After going to college and getting a degree in music management, Chris took a winding road to break into the music business. He took his first step into that world while still a university student by getting an internship at an Atlanta radio station, Hot 97.5.

At Hot 97.5, Chris became a student of the music industry and began making a name for himself. When people at the station started to recognize his talents for rapping and performance, they allowed him to rap on station promotions. A fan base developed, and Chris worked his way up to being a DJ.

As a radio personality, Chris became known as Chris Lova Lova. He was skilled with a mic and a favorite at the station. One of his signature marks was to rap his own lyrics to the hits that were being played, and his antics earned him a strong following. He jokes that he became "a ghetto celebrity." As a DJ, he was reaching a large audience for the first time. As his popularity grew, he got a gig producing a popular night show, and the exposure he got as Chris Lova Lova would eventually act as a launching pad for his own independent music career.

While earning his degree in music management, Chris worked for station Hot 97.5 in Atlanta. It wasn't long before rap fans found Chris, and the station made him a DJ. His fame and popularity continued to grow, and Chris Lova Lova became a local celebrity.

Ludacris Is Born

After working for three years as Chris Lova Lova, winning a local fan base, and saving enough money, Chris was ready to produce his own album. To do so, he decided he needed a new persona. Chris Lova Lova was a great radio DJ, but he wasn't a hip-hop star. The name Chris

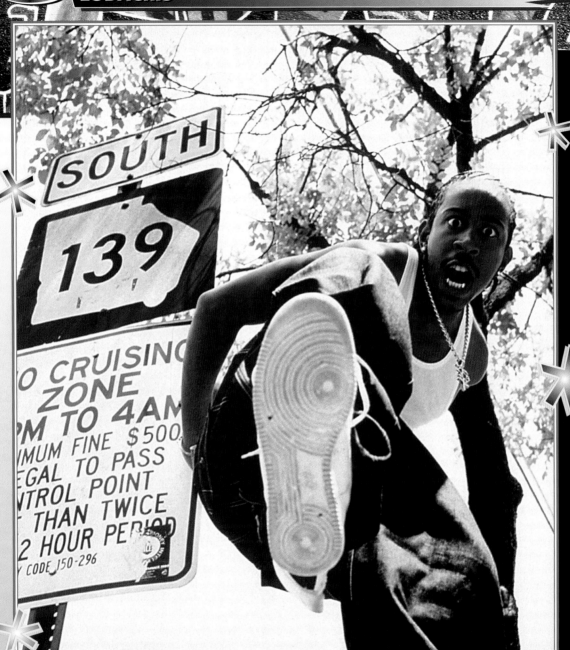

Chris Bridges hip-hop star needed his own identity, and he decided on Ludacris. The name reflects the two sides of Chris's personality—calm and collected but crazy; and describes his music—ludicrous lyrics and performances. Whatever the reasons behind it, the name is unforgettable.

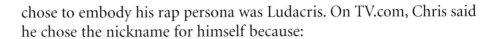

chose to embody his rap persona was Ludacris. On TV.com, Chris said he chose the nickname for himself because:

> **"I have kind of a split personality—part of me is calm, cool, and collected, while the other side is just beyond crazy. My lyrics are ludicrous, my live shows are ludicrous—ludicrous like off-the-chain crazy."**

Chris was a music management major and a radio DJ. He knew the realities of a self-produced album. It was an independent venture that most music-industry **moguls** would say can't succeed. Recording studios put huge amounts of money and an entire machine of marketing, image creation, promotion, and distribution behind an album. Even with all that support, many albums and artists still can't get a foot in the door when it comes to getting the public's attention. For people doing it all on their own, the prospects are infinitely worse. If their music is good, they might get a few local fans, even some limited regional radio play. But chances are they will never make back the money they spent on the venture.

Knowing all this, Chris "Ludacris" Bridges took the plunge and sunk his savings into producing his own album. It was 1999, and the album was called *Incognegro*. Against all odds and despite having to do virtually all his own marketing and distribution, the album became hugely popular in the southern music scene. Chris sold the albums for seven dollars apiece, mostly out of the trunk of his car, a 1992 Acura Legend, which he still drives because it "keeps me grounded." He sold an astonishing 50,000 albums. Suddenly, the music industry stood up and took notice of the local sensation known as Ludacris.

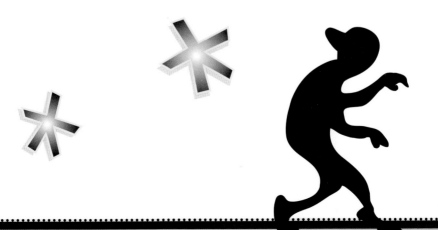

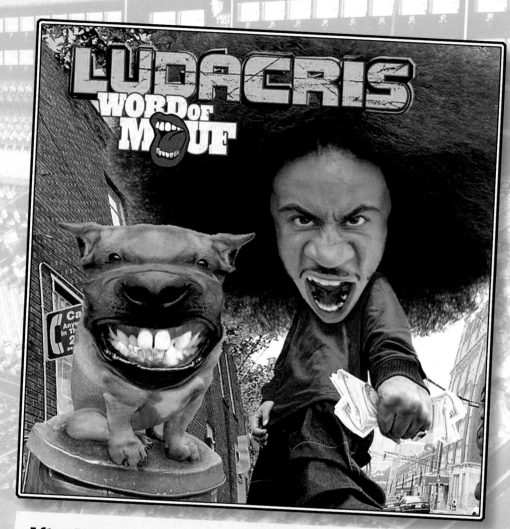

After Ludacris's successful debut, he was signed to a record contract by the legendary Def Jam Records. *Word of Mouf* brought Ludacris new fans from the popular music world. Now he was well known outside of the South.

3

Making It Big as Ludacris

After Ludacris made his huge independent **debut** in the southern market, Def Jam Records, a major hip-hop recording studio, knew they wanted him on board. Ludacris signed with the label in 2000, and his *Incognegro* album was repackaged and re-released as *Back for the First Time*. The album went triple platinum, and Ludacris's name and music were suddenly known nationwide.

The studio created a new imprint, Def Jam South, around their southern sensation. A year later, he was releasing his next album, *Word of Mouf*. With this album, Ludacris experienced his first mainstream "crossover" popularity. His songs were breaking out of the urban radio scene into the popular music world, a leap that is difficult for many of the more gritty hip-hop artists to make. But Ludacris's music was proving to have wide appeal. Like its predecessor, *Word of Mouf* went triple platinum.

Igniting Conservative Rage

With growing mainstream popularity came new opportunities . . . and new critics. That year, Ludacris made a deal with Pepsi. Music from Ludacris's popular single "Move Bitch" of the *Word of Mouf* album was used in a Pepsi commercial. It was great exposure for Ludacris, and Pepsi felt the use of the music connected the company and their product to and made them relevant with the young, urban market.

Not everyone saw the partnership as Ludacris and Pepsi saw it. Bill O'Reilly, a **conservative** television personality on Fox, found the situation particularly distasteful. He complained loudly that Pepsi was negatively influencing America's youth by collaborating with a "gangsta rapper" who used profanity, violence, and explicit sexuality in his rhymes. O'Reilly urged a boycott of Pepsi products.

Ludacris's music was quickly dropped from Pepsi's ad campaign, but in a somewhat **ironic** turn of events, the Osbourne family was signed instead. This enraged some in the Ludacris camp, because the Osbourne family is also famous for its use of profanity, history of drug use, and other attitudes and behaviors that conservatives like O'Reilly would find highly objectionable. Pepsi's choice of an equally controversial partner led those who supported Ludacris, particularly Russell Simmons, one of the Def Jam producers, to declare Pepsi **hypocritical** and perhaps even racist. In an interview with AskMen.com, Ludacris made the following comments about the situation:

> **"I just feel like O'Reilly is a racist. Definitely a hypocrite. I don't feel as if Pepsi values the black dollar. It's bigger than me. I don't feel that Pepsi values the black dollar because of what they did."**

Bill O'Reilly wasn't the only conservative media figure to take issue with Ludacris and his music. Bernard Goldberg, a former CBS reporter, also spoke out against Ludacris and the impact his type of music was having on America's youth. In 2005, Goldberg published a book called *100 People Who Are Screwing Up America*. In his book, Goldberg lists Ludacris as number sixty and gives him partial credit for the creation of disruptive American youth.

Those who support Ludacris or who do not subscribe to the beliefs espoused by people like Bill O'Reilly and Bernard Goldberg point out that the vision such men have of America—a vision in which America is a country governed by Christian values and morality, where all people who work hard can achieve the American dream, and where up until recently young people were motivated, respectful, upstanding young citizens—is actually a myth.

Those who take this side of the argument suggest that because people like Bill O'Reilly and Bernard Goldberg are wealthy, white, privileged men, they can live a comfortable existence, **insulated** by their wealth and beliefs. As a result, they never see the other side of America, the side marred by racism, poverty, broken dreams, and

Along with new, more mainstream fans came new critics, especially from the more conservative element of society. Pepsi quickly dropped Ludacris's music from one of its commercials when Fox television talk-show host Bill O'Reilly complained about the lyrics.

despair. The American dream has never existed for the poor and marginalized, and these young people never had the opportunity to become the type of citizens O'Reilly and Goldberg believe they should be. This is the side of America where many hip-hop artists like Ludacris grew up, and this is the reality they express in their art. These artists say they won't be **cowed** by conservative critics who are simply ignorant of their world.

Fighting Back at the Critics

Ludacris didn't let his critics, right wing or otherwise, put his music or message on hold. And he didn't permit them to take their shots without him fighting back either. In 2003, he released his next studio album, *Chicken N Beer*. It debuted at number one on the *Billboard* 200 album chart, and it had a little something for everyone, including something for his critics.

One of the singles on the *Chicken N Beer* album, "Blow It Out," is a response to Ludacris's critics, particularly Bill O'Reilly. Ludacris even mentions his conservative **nemesis** by name in the song. He raps:

> **" Shout out to Bill O'Reilly, I'm a throw you a curve**
> **You mad cause I'm a Thief and got away with words "**

"Blow It Out" as a song and as a video was different from the type of music Ludacris's fans were used to. His albums contain many upbeat, lighthearted songs that are accompanied by colorful, sexy videos. The video for "Blow It Out," in contrast, had a harsh, low-budget look more appropriate to the anger and **defiance** at the heart of the song.

The most successful single on *Chicken N Beer*, however, wasn't Ludacris's shout out to his critics. It was the immensely popular hit "Stand Up." The song was Ludacris's biggest crossover hit, and it went to number one on the *Billboard* Hot 100 chart. It was also featured on the soundtrack to the hip-hop dance movie *Honey*. *Chicken N Beer* went double platinum, selling over two million copies to date, making it Ludacris's third multi-platinum album in a row.

The Red Light District

In 2004, Ludacris released *The Red Light District*, his fifth studio album. Many critics felt it was a departure from his previous albums, revealing

HE'S THE MAN WITH THE DIRTIEST MOUTH IN THE GAME. BUT DON'TCHA LOVE HIM FOR IT? BOW DOWN TO THE KING OF COMEDY...

MUCH MORE MOUF

Feature zone: Ludacris. Words: Hattie Collins.

If critics such as Bill O'Reilly thought they could put an end to Ludacris's career, or at least make the artist change how he did things, they could not have been more wrong. He refused to compromise his beliefs to please others.

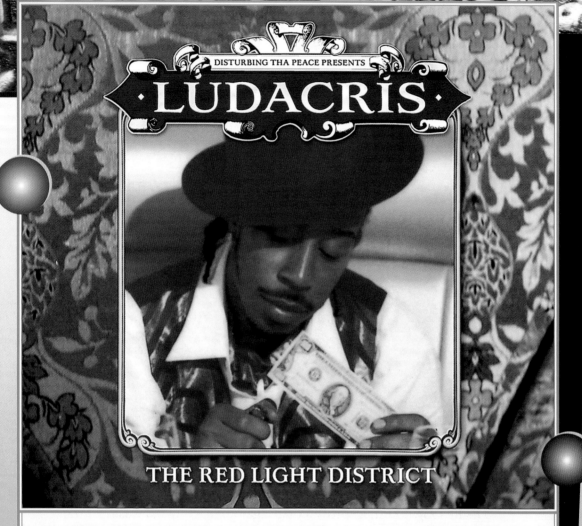

DISTURBING THA PEACE PRESENTS

·LUDACRIS·

THE RED LIGHT DISTRICT

In 2004, Ludacris released *Red Light District*, which some thought referred to a section in Amsterdam where drugs and prostitution are legal. Not so, says Ludacris. According to him, the title refers to a state of mind with no limitations.

an artist who had gained in maturity. Like *Chicken N Beer*, the album debuted at number one on the *Billboard* 200 album chart. When hearing the album's title, which is also a reference to Amsterdam's Red Light District, famous for its legalized prostitution and drugs, some people assume it is just another rap album filled with vulgar glorifications of

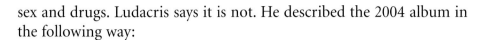

sex and drugs. Ludacris says it is not. He described the 2004 album in the following way:

> **"I think that with every album you have to give people a piece of you, something that they don't know about; whether it's personal or maybe a sound or idea they haven't heard before. That's something I set out to do this time. I know that the first thing people think of when they hear Red Light District is Amsterdam, but I'm referring to a state of mind. Where there are no limitations to what I can say, or I can do. On this album I talk about everything. I get personal about my emotions, money situations, my life. I've got metaphoric songs, club songs, songs for the women, party songs, songs about my experience traveling: just living my life. I really think this is my best album because it's what I've always wanted to do."**

In *The Red Light District*, Ludacris again took the opportunity to make a dig at his number-one critic, Bill O'Reilly. In the single "Number One Spot," Ludacris has some fun rhyming about O'Reilly's legal troubles. The conservative television personality became embroiled in his own controversy that year when one of his employees sued him for sexual harassment. Ludacris jibes, "Hi Mr. O'Reilly/Hope all is well, kiss the plaintiff and the wifey."

The Red Light District proved once again that Ludacris was the king of the Dirty South and one of hip-hop's heavy hitters. Like his other albums, *The Red Light District* became a multi-platinum hit, selling more than two million copies to date.

Getting the Respect and Recognition

His numerous successful albums have earned Ludacris fans and fame. They've also brought him numerous awards and **accolades**. In June 2004, Ludacris won BET's Viewer Choice award. In December of that same year, he won the MIB Hip-Hop Artist of the Year Award at the Ninth Annual Prism Awards. In August of 2005, the video for his single, "Number One Spot," earned an MTV Music Award for Best Rap Video. These are just some of the honors Ludacris has received.

However, the highest honor in the music world's award circuit is undoubtedly the Grammy. Ludicrous has won one of the coveted awards and been nominated for eleven others. His first Def Jam album, *Back for the First Time*, catapulted Ludacris onto the Grammy Award nomination list. That album was nominated for Best Rap Album in 2001—a high honor, especially for a debut artist.

The next year brought Ludacris two more Grammy nominations. One was for Best Rap/Sung Collaboration for the hit single "Area Codes," which featured hip-hop artist Nate Dogg. The other nomination was for Best Short Form Music Video for the single "One Minute Man."

In 2003, Ludacris was nominated for another two Grammy Awards: Best Rap Album for *Word of Mouf* and Best Male Rap Solo Performance for the single "Roll Out (My Business)." In 2004, he was nominated for three more Grammys: Best Song Written for a Motion Picture, Television Special for "Act a Fool," Best Rap Performance by a Duo or Group for "Gossip Folks" with Missy Elliot, and Best Male Rap Solo Performance for "Stand Up."

Ludacris's first Grammy win came in 2005. He won for Best Rap/Sung Collaboration for the hit "Yeah" with Usher and Lil Jon. "Yeah" also earned him nominations for Record of the Year and Best R&B Song. In 2006, Ludacris was nominated for one Grammy: Best Rap Solo Performance for "Number 1 Spot."

Despite the Grammy nominations and other awards, some of his fans feel Ludacris isn't getting the recognition he deserves. They complain that his only Grammy win is for a **collaborative** work; they insist he should be receiving awards for his solo singles; and they hint that he's being treated unfairly because he's a Dirty South rapper. Ludacris, however, isn't complaining. He's right where he wants to be: on top of the world.

Release Therapy

For Ludacris, all awards and accolades come second to the music. It's nice to be recognized, but it's better to produce good music whether or not it wins awards. Ludacris is staying focused on the quality of his music as he works on his much-anticipated fifth album, *Release Therapy*. The album is due out sometime in 2006. The album will complete his contract with Def Jam records, and it is unclear whether Ludacris will go on to produce more music with

The success Ludacris found with Def Jam brought him fans and awards. In 2005, he received the MTV Video Music Award for Best Rap Video for "Number One Spot." In the song, Ludacris rhymes about some legal difficulties Bill O'Reilly experienced.

(or without) the label. In talking about his upcoming album with MTV, he spoke of the significance of the title:

> **"The name *Release Therapy* is for two reasons. [For one thing,] I signed a five-album deal with Def Jam, and this is my fifth album. . . . You can count on your hand artists that've made it this far. I just feel good about it. It's one of those things that's therapeutic just to know I've made it this far. Depending on whether or not I want to continue going is up to me."**

Ludacris is soft-spoken, polite, and never afraid to say what is on his mind. This makes him a media favorite, and he never shies from talking to the press, as shown in this 2005 photograph.

Ludacris recognizes that all his success has now given him a world of options. Rapping has been his passion since he was a little boy, but he now has the fame, money, and soon the freedom to pursue other passions and find other outlets and uses for his creativity. He knows that few people are so lucky. He goes on, however, to explain the second reason for the upcoming album's name:

"Music is therapeutic. When I say *Release Therapy*, I just mean in what I do and speaking out. It is my release therapy, music, period. Every album I get more and more personal, start talking about issues that people would be surprised about or maybe didn't think I would say. I'm about to release. You can't keep stuff balled in. I never have kept stuff balled in, but I'm getting more and more comfortable talking [about] anything and just what's on my mind. That's what music is all about. Hopefully with me saying all of that . . . you understand the title."

His words about his upcoming album could be used to sum up his entire music career. From the time he was a child, music was a way Ludacris could understand and participate in the world. In the end, for him, the music—and getting his message out to an audience—is the most important thing.

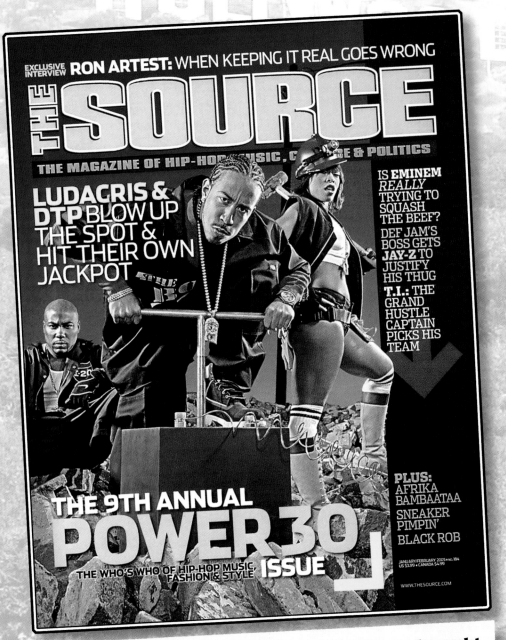

EXCLUSIVE INTERVIEW RON ARTEST: WHEN KEEPING IT REAL GOES WRONG

THE SOURCE

THE MAGAZINE OF HIP-HOP MUSIC, CULTURE & POLITICS

LUDACRIS & DTP BLOW UP THE SPOT & HIT THEIR OWN JACKPOT

IS **EMINEM** *REALLY TRYING TO SQUASH THE BEEF?*

DEF JAM'S BOSS GETS **JAY-Z** TO JUSTIFY HIS THUG

T.I.: THE GRAND HUSTLE CAPTAIN PICKS HIS TEAM

THE 9TH ANNUAL
POWER 30 ISSUE

THE WHO'S WHO OF HIP-HOP MUSIC, FASHION & STYLE

JANUARY/FEBRUARY 2005 • NO. 184
US $3.99 • CANADA $4.99

WWW.THESOURCE.COM

PLUS:
AFRIKA BAMBAATAA

SNEAKER PIMPIN'
BLACK ROB

Ludacris's multimillion-dollar–selling albums brought him to the top of the hip-hop world, as seen in this *The Source* cover from 2005. They also brought him the opportunity to expand his talents elsewhere, including acting.

4

Seizing the Day

With the fame of being a successful rapper came new opportunities, including offers for roles in movies. Although Ludacris wanted to try his hand at acting, he was hesitant at first. He knew that music stars who tried to become actors—and actors who tried to become music stars—could end up humiliating themselves. He need not have worried.

Ludacris's first appearance in a movie was as a customer in the 2001 hip-hop movie *The Wash*, starring Dr. Dre and Snoop Dogg. Ludacris's next acting role was larger and came in the 2003 hit movie *2 Fast 2 Furious*, the sequel to the 2001 movie *The Fast and the Furious*. Much larger roles, however, were still to come.

To the Academy Awards

Ludacris's greatest acting success to date is undoubtedly his performance in *Crash*, a 2005 movie about race relations in Los Angeles. Ludacris stars alongside some of the biggest names in the business, including Don Cheadle, Sandra Bullock, Matt Dillon, Brendan Fraser, Terrence Howard, and Larenz Tate. In the film, Ludacris plays Anthony, a car-jacker whose philosophizing on everything from music to the crimes he's committing makes the audience realize that concepts like "good" and "evil" are far more complicated than they initially seem.

Whereas in his previous films, Ludacris played characters that were basically self-portrayals, with the role of Anthony, he had to become a real actor. For the first time, Ludacris was playing a deep and compli-cated character who differed in many ways from himself. One of those ways shows in an ironic scene in which Anthony bashes hip-hop music and bemoans its influence on African Americans. He says the white **establishment** invented hip-hop to make African American arts and culture look stupid. Anthony goes on to say that every self-respecting African American should listen to country music.

To play a character like Anthony, Ludacris had to put aside his ego and become a student again. But Ludacris believed in *Crash* and its message, and he didn't find it hard to put aside his own beliefs about music and hip-hop and learn to embrace his character. His costar Terrence Howard was deeply impressed, and remarked in an interview with MTV:

> **"[Ludacris] came in there as a star, but he wanted to be treated as a pupil. . . . He asked for advice on every part of this thing. He let me beat him in the street for three, four hours because [the director] is such a perfectionist. We could have done it in ten minutes, but he withstood that. I have the utmost respect for Chris Bridges the actor."**

Howard's words mean a lot to Ludacris, who takes his acting so seriously that he wants his original name, Chris Bridges, used on his acting work. His performance in *Crash* earned him the right to be proud. It made huge waves in the movie industry and profoundly impacted its viewers. It was also the winner of Best Picture at the 2006 Academy Awards. After *Crash* won, Ludacris remarked of the film, "We freed a lot of people and a lot of minds, and that's why it was so powerful that it had to win Best Picture."

In the Oscar-winning film *Crash*, Ludacris plays Anthony (shown here with Larenz Tate, who played Peter), who doesn't like the influence hip-hop has on African Americans. Because he wants to be taken seriously as an actor, he often uses the name Chris "Ludacris" Bridges.

Ludacris has another reason to be proud about his performance in *Crash*. In January 2006, he and his cast mates won a Screen Actors Guild award for Outstanding Performance by an Ensemble Cast in a Motion Picture. What's more, his portrayal of Anthony in *Crash* wasn't Ludacris's only critically acclaimed acting role of 2005.

The 2005 film *Crash* was a hugh success and the actors formed a special bond. Here, Chris, Matt Dillon, Don Cheadle, and Terrence Howard show off their awards as winners of the Screen Actors Guild Award for Outstanding Performance by a Cast in a Motion Picture.

More Big-Screen Kudos

Within mere months of his breakout performance in *Crash*, Ludacris was receiving praise for his acting abilities again, this time for the movie *Hustle and Flow*. Another serious film, *Hustle and Flow* is about DJay (played by Terrence Howard), a pimp and drug dealer who dreams of making it big as a rapper. Ludacris plays the role of Skinny Black, a rapper who achieves fame but loses himself in Hollywood's materialistic world of fame and fortune.

The lives of rappers and pimps may seem a world away to a lot of people viewing the film, but Ludacris doesn't think people should consider their lives as so far apart. In fact, he believes that most people could find some common ground between their own lives and the

Chris costars with Terrence Howard in *Hustle and Flow* as a hometown rapper who found success in the hip-hop world. Howard plays a rap "wannabe," who wants Chris's character to listen to his demo tape. Though Chris's screen time is short, it's an important role.

lives of the characters he and Terrence Howard portray. He stated in an MTV interview:

> **"Everybody has a hustle. I don't care who you are; you have a hustle in your life no matter what you do. Whether it's your job or if it's a side-hustle; it's all about doing something to get what you have to get in life."**

Being able to find the common ground between himself and his character is one of the things that have led to Ludacris's recent acting success. He hopes there will be more success in this arena in the future. He is currently looking at other feature film scripts. He also recently played a killer in an episode of one of his favorite TV shows, *Law and Order, SVU.*

On Top as CEO

Most people hope to become successful in just one career. Ludacris already has a successful career as a rapper and as an actor. But he has another successful career as well. He never forgot the lessons he learned as a music management major, and now he's putting those lessons to good use as the head of an independent record label.

Ludacris told VH1, "I'm always trying to position myself to where I'm broadening my horizons." True to his word, he has enthusiastically seized every opportunity that fame and fortune have brought his way— and one of his biggest opportunities was the chance to become **CEO** of Disturbing Tha Peace Records, known also as DTP. In his important business role, he is helping to build the careers of other artists, including Fate, I-20, Shawnna, Playaz Circle, Tity Boi, and Bobby Valentino.

DTP has surprised people by signing artists outside the world of hip-hop. When discussing the studio's next compilation album in an MTV interview, Ludacris spoke of this variety as a strength for the company:

> **"With DTP, we never want to be limited to what we do. This compilation is showing how broad of a company we are. Not only do we have rap artists, but we surprised people by branching out and breaking a R&B artist, which is Bobby [Valentino]. This compilation will be showcasing what's to come and shock people even more [about] what they think we can and can't do. It's coming full throttle."**

Ludacris has put his music management degree to work as well. As CEO of Disturbing Tha Peace Records, he is giving young artists such as Bobby Valentino (seen here with Ludacris at the 2004 Prism Awards) a helping hand in the music world.

In a return to his radio roots, in 2005, Ludacris announced that he would host an XM Satellite Radio show. When he appeared at NASDAQ with XM CEO Hugh Panero, Ludacris became the first hip-hop artist to ring the stock exchange's opening bell.

Coming Full Circle

Full throttle is a good way to describe just about everything Ludacris does. And as if being a rapper, actor, and CEO weren't enough, he is now going to have his own show on XM Satellite Radio.

In September 2005, when the deal was announced, Ludacris appeared with XM Satellite Radio executives at NASDAQ headquarters and became the first hip-hop artist ever to ring the New York Stock Exchange's opening bell. Clearly, Ludacris is a force to be reckoned with, both in music and in business.

His new show will bring his career full circle: from Atlanta radio DJ to satellite radio host. Ludacris told Sirius Satellite Radio, "It feels real good to be back to it." He said pairing with XM, "was the perfect opportunity because it's raw and uncut. I'm a raw and uncut type of individual. So I think it's a perfect marriage."

Ludacris's show will be called *Disturbing Tha Peace Presents Ludacris' Open Mic*. Ludacris plans to use the show as a **forum** to feature artists from all regions; he also says there will be exclusive freestyles. It's just one more way that he will reach fans and give them something they can't find anywhere else.

When reflecting on all the opportunities he has had, Ludacris himself seems hardly able to believe it. He told MTV, "I don't understand how I've done all this stuff. . . . I've done more [in one year] than most people do in their lives, and I'm feeling good."

Early in his career, Ludacris began the Ludacris Foundation to inspire young people, empower families, and help community development. Headed by his mother, Roberta Shields, the foundation has helped many people get the tools they need to reach their dreams.

"HELPING YOUTH HELP THEMSELVES."

5

The Greater Good

Many celebrities say that the greatest thing about achieving fame and fortune is that their success makes them influential with the public and brings them close to powerful people, putting them in a position to help others. Chris "Ludacris" Bridges is no exception, and he seizes the opportunity to use his talents, fame, and fortune to help other people.

His own personal success isn't the only thing important to Ludacris. He's an artist who always has his mind on a higher goal. Ludacris hopes he can change both music and the world, and believes all artists should have similar goals. In several interviews, he has stated, "I'm in the game to change music. I think that's what every artist should be in it for. I'm here to change the world or as Tupac said, spark the brain that changes the world."

One of Ludacris's top concerns is building young people's self-esteem and providing opportunities for them, particularly young people who are considered "at risk," who are growing up in neighborhoods gripped by poverty and crime. To achieve his goals, he works with his own foundation and with other organizations.

The Ludacris Foundation

In association with William Engram and Chaka Zulu, Chris Bridges began the Ludacris Foundation in 2001 with the vision to "inspire youth to live their dreams, uplift families and foster economic development in the community." Chris Bridges is the foundation's chairman and CEO, and his mother, Roberta Shields, is the foundation's president. The foundation's mission statement is:

> **❝To show young people they are the architects of their future and instill our 'Principles of Success'—a roadmap for achieving dreams. To connect with our youth to build stronger families and communities.❞**

The foundation promotes eight "Principles of Success." They are self-esteem, spirituality, communication, education, leadership, goal setting, physical activity, and community service—all elements that have been important to Ludacris's own life and success. The foundation conducts its work through programs carried out by its own workers and volunteers and by providing grants to other organizations.

To date, the Ludacris Foundation has awarded more than half a million dollars in grants to organizations that provide opportunities to young people. It also currently runs five programs, including the "Stand-Up Initiative," which provides music, gifts, outings, and surprise visits to youth with disabilities; "Luda Cares," which provides toys, food, and clothing to children and their families; and "Healthy Lifestyle," which provides education on healthy eating and living to youth ages eight to fourteen.

The work done by the Ludacris Foundation is getting noticed. In October 2004, Ludacris and his foundation were honored, along with fellow hip-hop artist Mary J. Blige, the Anheuser Busch, Inc., and MTV's "Choose or Lose Campaign," at a benefit dinner in New York City. The awards benefit dinner raised money for the network, and Reverend Al Sharpton made the keynote speech. In 2005, the NBA Wives Association honored Roberta Shields, president of the foundation and Chris's mother, as an Outstanding Role Model. She had a profound impact on her son's growth into a responsible and successful individual despite difficult circumstances, and she is now working to do the same for other children.

The Hip-Hop Summit Action Network

One of the organizations Ludacris has worked with in the hopes of bringing about positive changes in the lives of young people is the Hip-Hop Summit Action Network (HSAN). HSAN describes its mission in the following way:

> **"Founded in 2001, the Hip-Hop Summit Action Network (HSAN) is dedicated to harnessing the cultural relevance of Hip-Hop music to serve as a catalyst for education advocacy and other societal concerns fundamental to the well-being of at-risk youth**

Ludacris and the Ludacris Foundation also work with HSAN. In this 2004 photo, Reverend Run, Mary J. Blige, Ludacris, Roberta Shields, C. Virginia Fields, and Russell Simmons attend the Hip-Hop Summit Action Awards Benefit Dinner.

throughout the United States. HSAN is a non-profit, **non-partisan** national coalition of Hip-Hop artists, entertainment industry leaders, education advocates, civil rights proponents, and youth leaders united in the belief that Hip-Hop is an enormously influential agent for social change which must be responsibly and **proactively** utilized to fight the war on poverty and injustice. **"**

Amid his busy life as a musician, businessman, actor, and radio personality, Ludacris makes sure to save time for one of his most important roles—father. In 2006, he and daughter Karma attended Nickelodeon's Kids' Choice Awards.

The major focuses of HSAN are promoting literacy and equal access to high-quality public education, supporting freedom of speech, encouraging voter education and involvement, facilitating economic advancement, and providing youth leadership development. To these ends, the organization has held more than forty summits in cities all over the United States, registered thousands of young people to vote, held protest rallies that have drawn tens of thousands of participants, helped protect public-education budgets and raise awareness of New York's Rockefeller drug laws, and partnered with numerous other organizations such as the NAACP, the National Urban League, and the Southern Christian Leadership Conference.

Looking to the Future

With a music career, an acting career, a record label, and a charitable foundation, it might seem like Ludacris would run out of time or energy. But as he moves into the future, he feels he has plenty of both—and he intends to use them well. Whether it's making music, acting in movies, building the careers of other artists through DTP, or improving the lives of children, Chris "Ludacris" Bridges intends to keep making a difference. He told contactmusic.com:

> **"I always tell people that longevity is the most important thing to me, so with that being said I've never looked back. I'm always looking forward. I know that when it comes to hip-hop, I'm one of the chosen few, and I'm very happy with that success. But as far as where I'm going, I have no limitations. . . . I'm just getting started."**

1970s   Hip-hop is born in the Bronx, New York.

1977   Christopher Bridges is born in Champaign, Illinois, on
         September 11.

1989   Joins his first hip-hop group, the Loudmouth Hooligans.

1990s   The hip-hop style known as Dirty South develops.

1999   Self-produces his first album, *Incognegro*.

2000   Signs with Def Jam Records.

2001   Acts in his first film, *The Wash*.

         Establishes the Ludacris Foundation.

         Hip-Hop Summit Action Network is formed.

         Receives his first Grammy nomination.

2004   The Ludacris Foundation is honored for its work.

         Wins awards from BET, Prism, and MTV.

2005   Creates controversy by wearing a Confederate flag while
         performing at the VIBE Awards.

         Is ranked number sixty in Bernard Goldberg's book *100 People
         Who Are Screwing Up America*.

         The NBA Wives Association honors Ludacris's mother,
         Roberta Shields, for her work with the Ludacris Foundation
         and her role in her son's life.

         Receives critical acclaim and a Screen Actors Guild award
         for his performance in *Crash*, as well as accolades for his
         role in *Hustle and Flow*.

         Wins his first Grammy Award.

2005   Signs a deal to host his own show on XM Satellite Radio, and
         becomes the first hip-hop artist to ring the New York Stock
         Exchange's opening bell.

Discography
Solo Albums
1999   *Incognegro*

2000   *Back for the First Time*

2001   *Word of Mouf*

2003   *Chicken N Beer*

2004   *The Red Light District*

2006   *Release Therapy*

Number-one Singles
2003   "Stand Up" (with Shawnna)

Selected Television Appearances
2002   *Soul Food*

2003   *Hard Rock Live*; *Hip Hop Babylon 2*; *Later with Jools Holland*; *Players: Ludacris*; *Trina: The Making of a Diamond Princess*; *The Daily Show with Jon Stewart*; *The New Tom Green Show*; *Tinseltown TV*

2004   *40 Most Awesomely Bad Dirty Songs . . . Ever*; *Chappelle's Show*; *Fuse 100%*; *Saturday Night Live*; *The Shady National Convention*; *Total Request Live*; *Live with Regis and Kelly*; *The Late Late Show with Craig Kilborn*; *Last Call with Carson Daly*

2005   *Driven*; *Eve*; *Krank Yankers*; *Saturday Night Live*; *The Late Late Show with Craig Ferguson*; *The Oprah Winfrey Show*; *Tavis Smiley*; *Late Show with David Letterman*; *Jimmy Kimmel Live*; *Live with Regis and Kelly*; *Ellen: The Ellen DeGeneres Show*; *The Tonight Show with Jay Leno*

2006   *Law & Order SVU*

Film
2001   *The Wash*

2003   *2 Fast 2 Furious*

2003   *Lil Pimp*

2005   *Crash*

2005   *Hustle & Flow*

Video

2001   *Missy "Misdemeanor" Elliott: Hits of Miss E. The Videos,
       Volume 1*

2002   *American Rap Stars*

       Hip-Hop VIPs

2003   *Inside* 2 Fast 2 Furious

       Making Music with Ludacris

       Nas: Made You Look—God's Son Live

       Trick Daddy: Uncut

2005   *Ciara Goodies: The Videos and More*

       Ludacris: The Red Light District

       The Music of Shark Tale

       Rhythm City Volume One: Caught Up

Awards

2004   BET Awards: Viewers Choice Award

       Prism Awards: MIB Hip-Hop Artist of the Year

2005   MTV Music Awards: Best Rap Video

       Grammy Awards: Best Rap/Sung Collaboration
       (with Usher and Lil John)

2006   Screen Actors Guild Awards: Outstanding Performance
       by a Cast in a Motion Picture

Books

Chang, Jeff. *Can't Stop, Won't Stop: A History of the Hip-Hop Generation.* New York: St. Martin's Press, 2005.

DeRemer, Leigh Ann. *Contemporary Musicians: Profiles of the People in Music.* Farmington Hills, Mich.: Thomson/Gale, 2003.

Light, Alan. *The Vibe History of Hip-Hop.* New York: Three Rivers Press, 1999.

Oh, Minya. *Bling Bling: Hip Hop's Crown Jewels.* New York: Wenner Books, 2005.

Waters, Rosa. *Hip-Hop: A Short History.* Broomall, Pa: Mason Crest Publishers, 2007.

Magazines

Ali, Lorraine. "Totally Ludacris." *Newsweek*, December 6, 2004.

Caramanica, Jon. "Ludacris: It's Not All Jokes and Rhymes." *Teen People*, June 16, 2002.

Davis, Kimberly. "A Wild Ride with Ludacris." *Ebony*, October 1, 2005.

"5 Questions for Ludacris." *Ebony*, August 1, 2003.

"Ludacris: Rap Star Keeps Conquering Music While Enjoying Success as Actor." *Jet*, June 20, 2005.

Sinclair, Tom. "Fowlmouthed: Nobody Makes a Chump Out of Hip-Hop's Beer-swillin', Chicken-chompin' Jester." *Entertainment Weekly*, October 17, 2003.

Web Sites

Def Jam Recordings
www6.defjam.com/ludacris/home.php

Disturbing Tha Peace Records
www.dtprecords.com

The Ludacris Foundation
www.theludacrisfoundation.org

MTV online
www.mtv.com

VH1.com
www.vh1.com/artists/az/ludacris/motv.jhtml

accolades—expressions of high praise.

advocacy—active verbal support for a cause or position.

catalyst—someone or something that makes change happen.

CEO—chief executive officer; a company's highest-ranking officer.

chauvinistic—having the characteristics of a person with excessive or prejudiced loyalty to a particular gender.

collaborative—working with others.

conservative—in favor of keeping things the way they are.

controversial—provoking strong disagreement.

cowed—frightened someone into submission or obedience.

debut—presented for the first time.

defiance—bold refusal to obey or conform.

DJ—someone who plays recorded music for the entertainment of others; disc jockey.

establishment—a group of people who hold the power in a social group and dominate its institutions.

forum—a place for discussion.

funk—a type of music derived from jazz, blues, and soul, and is characterized by a heavy rhythmic bass and backbeat.

garnered—collected or accumulated.

genre—one of the categories into which artistic works can be divided on the basis of form, style, or subject matter.

hypocritical—showing hypocrisy, the false claim to having admirable principles, beliefs, or feelings.

insulated—protected from something unpleasant.

ironic—characterized by irony, an incongruity between what is expected to happen and what actually happens.

jams—sessions of making improvised music for practice, fun, or experimentation.

legitimacy—value as a serious art form.

longevity—the length of someone's life or career.

marginalized—prevented from having attention or power.

materialistic—concerned with physical wealth rather than spiritual and intellectual values.

MC—emcee; someone who acts as the master of ceremonies.

melded—various things blended to become one new creation.

metaphoric—having the characteristics of a metaphor, the use of a word that is not to be taken literally, but to be used to make a comparison.

mixer—a machine that takes multiple inputs and combines them to make a single output.

moguls—important and powerful people, often in media.

nemesis—a bitter enemy, especially one who seems unbeatable.

non-partisan—not belonging to or supporting any political party.

platinum—in music, singles that have sold more than one million copies or CDs that have sold two million.

proactively—done in a manner of acting rather than reacting to events.

quintessential—representing the typical example of something.

R&B—rhythm and blues; a blending of jazz and blues.

renaissance—renewal.

soul—music that originated in African American gospel singing and is characterized by strong feeling and earthiness.

synthesizers—computerized electronic tools for producing and controlling sound.

venues—locations.

Like Ludacris, **Celicia Scott**'s talents showed up early: Celicia has been a storyteller since she was three years old, and her first story was published when she was nineteen. Although Celicia confesses that she can't sing at all, she's enjoyed the chance to tell a singer's story.

Picture Credits

page

2: Zuma Press/Rena Durham
8: Jason Nelson /AdMedia/ Sipa Press
10: KRT/NMI
11: Piotr Redlinski/Sipa Press
13: KRT/NMI
15: KRT/Lionel Hahn
16: KRT/George Bridges
18: Michael Spleet/WENN
20: UPI Photo/John Hayes
23: NMI/Michelle Feng
25: WENN
26: Photofest
28: NMI/Def Jam Records

31: CE006/Ace Pictures
33: KRT/NMI
34: NMI/Michelle Feng
37: Zuma Press/NMI
38: Shannon McCollum/WENN
40: NMI/Michelle Feng
43: Lions Gate Films Inc./NMI
44: INFGoff/infusla-20
45: MTV Films/NMI
47: UPI Photo/Francis Specker
48: PRNewsFoto/NMI
50: Shannon McCollum/WENN
53: Zuma Press/Aviv Small
54: Zach Lipp/AdMedia

Front cover: PRNewsFoto/NMI
Back cover: KRT/NMI